First published in Great Britain in 1983 by
Macmillan Publishers Limited

This edition published in 1989 by
Treasure Press
Michelin House
81 Fulham Road
London SW3 6RB

ISBN 1 85051 368 6

Produced by Mandarin Offset
Printed and bound in Hong Kong

Editor: Miranda Smith
Designer: Julian Holland
Picture Researcher: Stella Martin
Photo Credits: All Sport Photographic 52-3, 69 below; Animal
Photography 22 above and below, 23, 50 below; BBC Hulton
Picture Library 69 above, 74 below, 76 above, 80; Jan Burgess
48; Bruce Coleman 8, 10, 11, 16-17, 43 above; Gerry Cranham
15, 75, 78-9, 85, 92-3; Jesse Davis 21, 54, 55, 67; Mary Evans
Picture Library 68; Steve Godfrey 30-9, 42, 43 below, 44-49; Kit
Houghton Photography 81 below; Alan Hutchison Library 2-3,
6-7, 12-13, 40, 62, 88-9, 92, 93; Bob Langrish 4-5, 14, 58, 64, 66,
70, 71 above, 72, 73, 74 above, 76 below, 82; Mansell Collection
56-7; Stuart Newsham 16, 51 above, 78, 81 above, 84, 90, 91;
Scala/Firenze 28-9; Spectrum 18-19, 51 below, 52, 71; Vision
International 25, 60-1, 86-7, 90-1; Peter Newark's Western
Americana 56; ZEFA 9, 10-11, 12, 17, 24-5, 26, 26-7, 27, 40-1,
59, 65, 83, 88, 94, 94-5
Cover picture: Animal Photography
Artwork: Garden Studios/Joan Thompson 33, 34, 35, 38, 39,
42, 44, 45, 48, 63, 77; Linden Artists/David Astin 20-1

Our special thanks to Malcolm Pyrah, and
also to Keith Adams, his staff and the pupils
of the Sawyers Hall Riding Establishment,
Brentwood, for their help and co-operation
in the making of this book.

The World of Horses

Jan Burgess

TREASURE PRESS

Contents

Introduction 5

Wild Horses 6

Breeds and Breeding 12

The Horse in War 28

Learning to Ride 30

Ceremonies 40

Behind the Scenes 42

A Job with Horses 50

The Spanish Riding School 54

Riding Western 56

Horses in Entertainment 64

Famous Horses 68

The Competition Horse 70

Index 96

A small boy and his pony enjoy a cooling bathe in the tropical forests of the Amazon. Horses have lived in human company for thousands of years, acting both as workers and friends.

Introduction

This book offers a valuable introduction to anyone who is interested in horses. Each aspect of the world of horses is clearly described, from evolution to equitation.

Riding is a rapidly expanding sport on all levels and in all its many spheres. An increasing number of people are able to enjoy hacking around the countryside, hunting and riding-club events; fewer have the talent and dedication necessary to compete at professional standard.

The World of Horses provides vital background information for people who are interested in horses on any level. For someone who would like to learn to ride, it explains what that entails and advises on how to select a good riding school. For someone who is already able to enjoy riding, it offers advice on stable management and safety on the roads (a point often overlooked). For the armchair horseperson, it describes the principles, rules and methods of scoring in the various types of competition. For those even more academically interested, *The World of Horses* includes a fascinating historical account of the horse.

Horses can provide a great deal of pleasure but they are also very hard work and a round-the-clock responsibility which should not be underestimated. This book will stimulate a deeper interest in readers and open their minds to all aspects of these fascinating, noble and courageous creatures. It is a pleasure and a privilege to be part of the world of horses.

Left: Malcolm Pyrah with his outstanding horse, Towerlands Anglezarke. Together they have had many successes. Most recently, they won the silver medal in the 1981 European Championships at Munich, and came second in the 1982 World Championships at Dublin.

Wild Horses

Over millions of years of evolution, horses have adapted to life on plains and grassland. They wander at will, browsing on grass and shrubs. They have developed sharp senses of smell and hearing, so that they know well in advance when danger threatens. If you have ever been lucky enough to watch a new-born foal, you will know that it struggles to its feet within minutes. Its long legs look quite out of proportion to its body, but they enable it to keep up with its mother, within hours of birth. This helps the whole herd to keep out of danger, for, by running fast, the group can escape its enemies. Even horses that have never known the wild stay on the lookout for danger. Quietly grazing in a field, horses will lift their heads from time to time, sniffing the air to check that there is nothing out of the ordinary.

Horses in the wild live in groups or herds. A number of females, or mares, and their young are led by a male, or stallion. Rival stallions often try to kidnap mares to add to their own herd. They fight fiercely, squealing, kicking and biting until one or the other is driven off. Within any group of horses there is always a pecking-order. Even within a group of riding horses, living in a field, one horse soon asserts himself as the boss. He will insist on first pick of any food, driving away the others, and this can lead to problems at meal-times!

Although a few horses survive in the wild, most are now reared on farms and in studs. However, even when horses have lived for generations in human company, they still retain their natural shyness. Only by careful training can the rider gain the trust of his horse. In the wild, a horse can gallop, jump and perform the most complicated dressage movements quite naturally. It is quite another matter to persuade him to do these things on demand and with a rider on his back.

The wild ponies in Mongolia wander over the semi-desert in search of grazing. They are rounded up from time to time, and young ponies are selected for riding.

Herds of Przewalski's horses are kept in zoos and wildlife parks. They are very similar to horses that survived the last Ice Age. They are dun-coloured which means they have sandy coats with dark manes, tails and lower legs. They may also have a dark stripe along their backs, like a donkey, and zebra stripes on their legs.

By examining fossils and comparing bones and teeth patterns, scientists have been able to find out some of the history of the horse. The ancestors of horses and ponies existed some 60 million years ago. However, you would not have recognized the tiny animal of prehistoric times, for it did not look much like today's horse. It was only about the size of a large dog, and it had pads instead of hooves.

Over a period of millions of years, there were extreme changes in climate. As the temperature and food-supply altered, many animals died out and new species developed. The ancestors of the horse grew gradually larger. They died out in some places, for example in America, but they thrived in others. When the first members of the human race appeared on earth, they were able to hunt herds of wild horses for food. About 30,000 years ago, prehistoric people painted pictures of thick-set, short-legged horses on the walls of caves in Lascaux, France. They were of different colours, sometimes with striped and spotted legs and backs.

A horse very similar to the ones in those prehistoric herds survives today. In 1881, a Russian explorer called Colonel Przewalski came across herds of small wild horses, roaming across the semi-desert steppes of Mongolia. Today, it is uncertain how many actually survive in the wild, for the Przewalski horse has been hunted for food by local tribesmen. However, a number have been bred in captivity and you can see them in zoos and wildlife parks. They are small, only the size of a large pony. Usually dun in colour, with dark mane, tail and legs, they are of stocky build with large, heavy heads.

These moorland ponies are well equipped to survive the cold of winter. Because they are quite small, they do not need much grazing. They grow thick, waterproof coats and bushy manes and tails. Ponies can survive cold, dry weather quite happily, but they do not like long periods of rain.

All animals adapt to suit the place and climate in which they live. Horses have managed to survive in the hot, dry deserts of the Middle East and Africa, as well as the snowy tundra of the sub-Arctic. In cold, inhospitable surroundings, where grazing is scarce, the primitive horses remained small. They grew thick coats and manes as a protection against the weather. In hot desert climates, thick coats were a disadvantage. The animals that survived best there had fine hair. They developed speed and stamina to travel long distances in search of food. In places where there were lush forests and plenty of vegetation, horses grew larger because there was plenty of food. They also tended to be slower-moving. Hidden by thick undergrowth, they could not use speed to run away from an enemy.

So, quite naturally, horses grew to different shapes and sizes in different parts of the world. They had different coat colours and different temperaments. These basic types are

Welsh ponies usually make good riding ponies. Breeders divide them into sections or groups depending on size.

10

the raw material from which all the different breeds and varieties we know today have grown.

It was not long before man began to take a hand in things. We know that the Chinese kept horses 4,000 years ago. Very soon, people realized that certain types of horses were good for certain types of work. Horses for pulling loads had to be muscular and powerfully built. Horses that dragged chariots into battle had to be bold, fast and quick to turn. A riding horse had to be a comfortable mount for many hours. It also had to have a long stride in order to cover the ground as quickly as possible.

Human children inherit the colour of their eyes and hair from their parents. In the same way, horses pass on their characteristics to their offspring. By choosing the stallions and mares from which to breed, it is possible to encourage these characteristics. So, as well as the types that grew up quite naturally, man has tried to 'improve' on nature. Some of the best-known breeds today have their origins way back in history. But often they have been deliberately changed. New blood has been introduced, perhaps to make the breed a little larger or to encourage a particular colour.

Above: These grey horses live in the marshy Camargue region of southern France. They are used to herd the black bulls that also roam the marshes. The foals are born almost black but their coats lighten in colour as they get older.

Right: Rival stallions fight each other fiercely to prevent any member of their herd from being stolen. These mustangs, as wild horses are known in America, were photographed near Wyoming.

Breeds and Breeding

One of the most ancient breeds of all is the Arabian horse. Horses that look very similar to today's Arab were painted on the walls of caves 2,000 years ago. It is still the most exquisite of horses with its silky coat, flowing tail and mane, and elegant build. The Arab horse evolved in hot dry deserts. It had to withstand great heat and be able to travel long distances in search of food and water.

Arab horses are bred all over the world today, and most of them have never seen a date palm! However, they show their desert ancestry in their fine silky hair, tough legs and feet and above all in their great stamina. Some old horsemen even say that Arab horses do not like to go through water, but this may just be an old wives' tale! Arabs are used for general riding and jumping but they have taken part most successfully in long-distance rides and endurance competitions.

Breed societies are usually set up to keep records of pedigrees and to lay down rules about the shape and size that the breed should be. Horses are usually measured in hands

Left: The height Arab breeders prefer for pure-bred Arabs is between 14.1 and 15.2 hands. You can usually tell whether a horse is an Arab or has some Arab blood in its veins by looking at its head. The face tends to be dished, or concave, when viewed from the side. The muzzle then flares out, giving the Arab the expression which distinguishes it from other breeds.

and inches (a hand is 10 centimetres or 4 inches). The height measurement is taken from the top of the withers – the bony point where the top of the neck runs into the shoulders – to the ground. Arabs are fairly small. To be registered with the breed society, they must range between 14.1 and 15.2 hands.

The Arab is certainly an important breed in its own right. It has also been crossed with other breeds to improve them. Many European and American breeds have Arab blood in their veins, from the heavily-built French cart-horse, the Percheron, to the lightly built New Forest pony. But probably the most famous breed to grow out of the Arab is the Thoroughbred.

Above: Horses of Arab type in their natural surroundings. Although they are comparatively small and lightly built, Arabs have enormous stamina. Despite their delicate appearance, they can carry grown men more successfully than many more heavily-built animals.

The Thoroughbred

The Thoroughbred is a fairly new breed but it is certainly an important one. It is the horse that you will always see on the racecourse, and in show jumping and eventing.

Thoroughbred simply means carefully bred. The story goes that all Thoroughbreds can trace their ancestry back to just three stallions. The first is known as the Byerley Turk, after Captain Byerley who captured it from the Turks and took it to Britain. The Darley Arabian was brought back in 1704 by Thomas Darley. The Godolphin Arabian came originally from the Sultan of Morocco. It was found pulling a cart on the streets of Paris, and was also taken to Britain. These three horses all went on to found breeding-lines which were outstandingly successful on the racecourse.

The General Stud Book was started in 1793. It records the details and parentage of all Thoroughbreds. Since those days, the English Thoroughbred has been exported all over the world. Winning racehorses command very high prices, so the breeding of Thoroughbreds is very big business.

Above: The Thoroughbred is built for speed. It is the breed that is always used for flat racing, and usually for racing over jumps as well. This colourful group makes a magnificent sight, racing down the Musselburgh course in Scotland.

Right: Most horses are not mature enough to be broken in and worked until they are four years old. At Thoroughbred breeding-centres, or studs, the foals are fed concentrated high-protein food right from the start. They grow quickly and are raced on the flat at just two years old.

Left: The Thoroughbred has been called the miracle horse. It has great speed, beauty and intelligence. It has been crossed with other breeds to produce horses ideal for jumping, eventing – in fact for many types of riding.

Ponies

Ponies are types of small horse which are below 15 hands high. Their body shape is also different from a horse, for their heads tend to be larger, and they are often stronger for their size than horses. Ponies survive all over the world, often in places where horses would not be able to find enough food. In cold countries, the ponies are stocky and grow thick winter coats. In tropical climates, they are usually smaller and more slightly built but still very tough.

Distinct breeds of pony developed naturally on islands or in isolated places where new stocks of animals could not easily be introduced. Many of the Indonesian Islands, for example, still depend on ponies for transport. The climate is hot and the grazing is poor but the native ponies are extremely strong and wiry.

Britain's climate is ideal for raising ponies with its mild winters and lush grazing in summer. There are nine different breeds – the New Forest, Dartmoor, Exmoor, Dales, Fell, Highland, Connemara, Shetland and Welsh. They range in size from the tiny Shetland to the larger Welsh ponies, so they make ideal mounts for all ages and

Above: The tiny Falabella comes from Argentina. It is the smallest breed. Mature animals range from about 12 to 40 ins at the shoulder. It is named after the man who founded the breed.

Right: The sturdy Fjord pony comes from Norway but is found throughout Scandinavia. It is dun or cream in colour. Like the horses of prehistoric times, it has a stiff, upright mane and a dark stripe along its back.

Left: Shetland ponies still roam the Shetland Islands of Scotland as they have done for 2,000 years. They are very strong and hardy, and grow thick woolly coats and manes in winter. To be registered with the breed society, mature Shetlands must not be more than 42 inches (small breeds are measured in inches not hands).

weight. In fact, British ponies have been exported all over the world and some are even bred overseas.

Each breed has its own breed society to look after its interests. The small Exmoor is the most ancient of Britain's breeds. Exmoors are usually dark in colour with light 'mealy' muzzles. Perhaps the most popular breed world-wide is the Welsh pony and cob. Breeders divide them into four sections. The smallest, section A, are not more than 12 hands. They are probably the original breed from which the larger animals have sprung. Section B ponies can be up to 13.2 hands and make ideal riding and jumping ponies. Section C ponies are more heavily built and are said to be of cob type, but still only up to 13.2 hands in height. Section D is the Welsh cob, which is up to 15.2 hands.

Heavy Horses

At shows and carnivals, it is the heavy breeds that always attract the crowds. People seem to be fascinated by the massive size and power of the heavies. Despite their size, they are usually willing and kind-natured.

Before the petrol-engine, heavy horses did all the farm-work and pulled heavy loads in towns. When machinery was introduced and petrol was cheap, horse-power went out of fashion. It looked as though the heavy breeds might even disappear. Now that oil prices are rising, a few farmers are going back to horse-power. There are a good many advantages. Horses live on oats, hay and grass – all easily available and cheap on a farm. Unlike tractors, horses stop and move forward on command and do not get bogged down in sticky wet clay. Once a tractor wears out, it goes on the scrap-heap. A mare can have a foal every year if necessary, with little effect on her own work.

The main heavy breeds come from Europe. They are also very popular in the United States, Canada and Australia, where they have been exported to start breeding-stocks. One of the oldest breeds is the Ardennes from France. It is smaller than most of the heavies – 15 to 16.3 hands – but massively built. The British breeds are the Shire, Clydesdale and Suffolk. The one you are most likely to see is the Shire. A big Shire weighs a tonne or more and may stand as high as 19 hands. In the old days, Shires had great cascades of hair or 'feather' on their lower legs. This was difficult to keep clean on a working horse, and today breeders prefer finer feather.

You can often see heavy horses in displays and shows. Heavies are always decorated for special occasions. The finely-worked harness is hung with horse brasses, and manes and tails are often braided with ribbons and bells. Some of these decorations once had a practical purpose – to keep off flies or warn people to keep out of the way.

A fine pair of Shires join in an Easter parade in London. Heavy horses are more economical than motor vehicles over short distances. They also act as marvellous advertisements, because everyone turns to look at them.

Colours and Markings

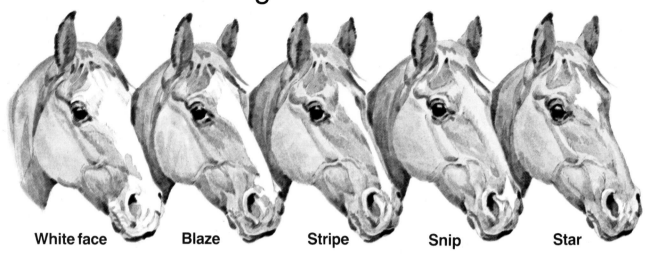

White face   Blaze   Stripe   Snip   Star

Although there are fashions in colours and markings, it is really the shape of the horse, not the colour, that matters. There are also all kinds of superstitions relating to coat colour. In the past, if a horse had four white legs it was thought to be a bad sign. One or two white legs was perfectly acceptable. Chestnuts are still thought to be fiery and excitable, and racehorse trainers sometimes dislike black horses because they have a reputation for being bad-tempered.

Apart from their coat colour, horses often have markings on their head and legs. White marks on the lower legs are called socks or stockings depending on how far they extend.

Chestnuts and bays are popular with exhibitors because their coats shine like silk when groomed. Chestnut varies from a light golden 'bright chestnut' to dark 'liver chestnut'. Bay ranges from rich, light brown to dark mahogany. Bays usually have dark 'points' – the mane, tail and lower legs.

Cleveland Bay

Bright chestnut Thoroughbred

Liver chestnut American quarter horse

Skewbald cob

Piebald pony

The palomino is not a breed but a colour. It has been called the golden horse of the West because it is popular in the United States. The palomino coat should be the colour of a 'newly-minted gold coin', or two shades lighter or darker.

Left: Many horses have markings on the head and lower legs, in contrast with the main coat colour. Chestnuts for example often have white markings. These marks are described very precisely by their own special terms. Some of the more valuable horses have 'passports' containing details of pedigree. An exact description of any body-marks is also included. This record helps to avoid questions of mistaken identity.

Black Percheron

Grey Lippizaner

Palomino

Dun pony

Roan New Forest pony

Appaloosa

Brown Shetland pony

American Breeds

The horse died out in America in prehistoric times. It was reintroduced in the 1500s by the Spanish invaders. The first breed to be developed in America was the Quarter horse. This is the real cowboy horse of the Wild West. It was bred from Arab, Barb and Turk horses crossed with English mares, all imported from Europe. It got its name because Quarter horses were used to run quarter of a mile races.

The Morgan breed was founded on a single stallion in the 1780s. This horse was named Morgan after its owner, Justin Morgan. Morgan was only 14.1 hands but tremendously strong. It helped its owner clearing trees on his farm, and could outpull far larger horses in competitions. Morgan founded a breed because its offspring looked exactly like their sire, no matter what the mares were like!

Other breeds include the Appaloosa, which is strikingly spotted or blotched. This type of horse was first popular with the Nez Percé Indians. Horses such as the American Saddlebred and Tennessee Walking Horse were developed for their comfortable or showy paces. The Standardbred was bred for racing at the trot. They got their name because they could only be registered if they covered a mile in a standard time of about 2½ minutes.

Above: The style of 'showing' horses in America is often very different from the European style. This Morgan is encouraged to stand very upright, with its hind legs extended. The Morgan is a small horse, between 14 and 15.2 hands, close-coupled and strong. Morgans are used as riding horses, for show-jumping, in harness and in long-distance riding.

Right: Quarter horses were used by the cowboys who drove cattle from one side of America to the other. They have endurance as well as the tremendous burst of speed necessary to cut out or round up a stray animal. At competitions and shows Quarter horses excel in the old sports of the cowboy era.

Left: The Saddlebred was developed for its smooth and comfortable paces. As well as the walk, trot and canter, Saddlebreds are taught to perform two further paces, the slow gait and the rack. Saddlebreds are always shown with their tails carried very high. This high position is achieved by cutting the muscle at the base of the tail.

Working Horses

When people talk about working horses, they mean in particular horses used to take them from place to place, and to carry or pull loads.

Until about a hundred years ago, horse-drawn vehicles were the most important means of transport. People first dared to get onto the backs of horses about 3,000 years ago. Before this they used horses to pull and carry, and to drag light chariots into battle. Gradually horse-breeders began to choose horses for their ability to do the job. This generally meant that the horses they chose were strong and muscular. They had to have tough legs and hooves that could stand up to jarring on rough surfaces for many hours. They had to be easily trained and patient enough to stand about while goods were loaded and unloaded. They also had to survive with the

Above: By tradition, gypsies have always kept horses. A nomadic people, they came originally from the Middle East. Horses pulled their homes and belongings from place to place.

Like the young of most grazing animals, foals are on their feet within minutes of birth. Wherever their dams go, the foals follow close by, as you can see in this photograph.

Right: Sleighs, or troikas, are drawn by horses in snow-covered Moscow. The horses are fitted with special shoes which help them keep their feet on the hard-packed snow.

minimum of special food and care. Of course, in working horses and ponies, looks and colouring are secondary to performance.

Heavy horses are the obvious workers of the horse world. Throughout history they have been bred for the greatest possible power and stamina. However, sturdy ponies can often pull greater loads, size for size, than the larger animals. They need less food, can survive worse weather and are more sure-footed on uneven ground. The little Austrian Haflinger was used in harness and as an agile pack pony on mountain trails. Even tiny Shetlands can carry full-grown men up and down mountainsides, tending sheep flocks. The ponies of the Greek Islands are slight and wiry and survive on the bare minimum of food. They are widely used on farms and small-holdings, fetching, carrying and tending the crops, managing the hilly terraces with ease.

Most horses and ponies have to work for their living in one way or another. With the high cost of grazing land and food, few people can afford to keep horses simply as pets. Although show-jumping, gymkhana games or simply going for a ride are sport for a rider, they are work for his mount.

Above: Before the invention of the petrol engine, horses did most of the farm work. They cleared the land, ploughed it, sowed and harvested the crops. Then they transported the produce to barns and granaries for storage. When a pair of horses are used, it is important that they should pull evenly. The horses are trained to stop, start, turn right and left on command. This leaves the driver's hands free for other jobs.

Above: Pack horses that work in such steep and stony terrain have to be sure-footed and strong. Horses not used to this kind of going would quickly go lame, straining their legs and bruising their feet on the uneven pathway. This pony and rider are resting as they travel through the mountains of Santa Cruz in South America.

Left: On the grasslands of South America, rearing beef cattle is the most important crop. The ranches cover hundreds of square kilometres, far too large to be divided up into fields. Over such vast distances, or in times of flood, motor vehicles cannot be used to check the stock.

The Horse in War

One of the first uses of the horse was to wage war. Harnessed to chariots, they gave the warrior speed and a steady platform from which to fight. Over the centuries, styles of warfare have come and gone. One of the most successful cavalries was the Mongol horde of Ghenghis

This picture of battling warriors probably sums up most people's idea of what the knight on his horse looked like. The scene was painted in about 1456 by Paulo Uccello, a

Florentine artist. The subject is the Battle of San Romano. The horses are not large, but they are powerfully built. The long spears were used to dislodge an enemy from his horse.

Khan. The Mongols rode small shaggy ponies that could hardly gallop, and they conquered a third of the earth's surface. At the other end of the scale was the medieval knight on his charger. Chargers had to be powerful enough to carry an enormous weight of armour into battle at the gallop.

Learning to Ride

You may be lucky enough to own your own pony. In this case, you probably learned to ride as soon as you could walk. Most people, however, learn to ride at a local riding school by going for a series of lessons. It is important to choose a good school. In Britain, riding establishments are inspected regularly by the British Horse Society and Ponies of Britain. If the school near you is 'approved' by either of these organizations, you are off to a good start.

You can also find out about a riding school by visiting it before you book your lessons. Does it look reasonably tidy and well kept? Are the people who run it helpful and interested? When you book a lesson, you should be asked about your weight and height and how much riding experience, if any, you have had. This information enables the school to choose a mount of the right size and temperament for your first trial on horseback.

Below: You must learn how to control your mount before you are safe to go out for a ride. When out on roads and lanes, riders always go in single file so that other traffic can overtake safely. The rider keeps to the left and uses hand signals for turning left or right. There are general road-safety tests for riders which everyone is encouraged to take.

Above: At a good riding school, lessons take place in an enclosed school called a manege. Working in an enclosed space ensures that the horse or pony cannot take charge while the rider is still unsure of how to control it.

Right: You will learn to control your pony from the ground as well as from its back. Ponies need kind but firm treatment, otherwise they soon learn how to get their own way. This young rider is leading her pony correctly from the left side. The reins are over the pony's head, not left hanging round its neck. The stirrups are safely run up the leathers. This ensures that they do not catch on gate-posts as the pony goes through.

Mounting and Dismounting

When you first begin to ride, there seem to be strict rules about everything. They are made mainly to ensure safety. Even a small pony is much stronger than an adult, so all horses and ponies must be treated with respect. Ponies get used to being handled from the left side. It is best to approach towards the left shoulder, never from behind. Never feed a riding school pony with titbits. This may sound unkind, but if a pony learns to expect titbits, it may start to snap at hands and pockets.

There is no need to buy expensive riding clothes to start with. Wear trousers that are not too tight, and tough shoes with a low heel that will not slip through the stirrups. Wellingtons and gym shoes are dangerous. A well-fitting hard hat is essential.

To mount correctly, first check the girths are tight. Stand close to the left shoulder, facing the tail. Take both reins and your stick (if you have one) in your left hand, close to the pony's withers. Steady the stirrup with your right hand, and place your left foot firmly into it.

Now twist or hop round so you are facing the saddle, but close to the pony's side. Put your right hand on the far side of the saddle. Spring up lightly, swinging your right leg over the pony's back. Make sure that you do not haul yourself up by pulling on the back of the saddle.

Land lightly in the saddle, without thumping down hard on the pony's back. Find your right stirrup. Take the reins in both hands. Check that the girths are still tight – you may have to take them up a hole or two. Be careful not to kick the pony in the sides or back while you are mounting.

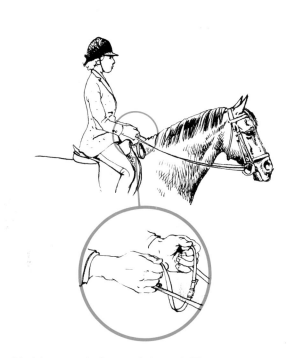

Hold one rein in each hand. The rein should go from the horse's mouth, between your little and third finger, and then out between your thumb and first finger. Your palms face inwards, with thumbs uppermost.

To dismount, the whole process is reversed. Take both feet out of the stirrups. Put both reins and stick in your left hand. Put your right hand on the front of the saddle and lean forwards slightly. Do not let the reins go into loops, or your pony may walk forwards.

In one movement, swing your right leg smoothly over the pony's back. Your weight will be resting on the front of the saddle. Be careful not to kick the pony in the back as you do this, but do not fling your leg too high up in the air either. Keep control of your mount so that it does not walk forward.

Allow your body to slide gently down the pony's side. Land lightly with your knees bent. Make sure you do not kick the pony's leg or you may have your toe trodden on rather heavily! Take hold of the reins or loop your arm through them while you loosen the girths and run up the stirrups.

Basic Riding Skills

Your first lesson may be on the lunge. This means that the pony is controlled by the instructor, who has a long line attached to the pony's bridle, and a whip. This allows the rider to concentrate on getting used to sitting on the pony, without having to worry about guiding it or controlling its pace. Early lessons are usually at walk and trot. The rider learns to absorb the movement of the horse by moving his own back and seat.

The rider sits in the lowest part of the saddle, with back straight. The legs are close to the pony's sides. The ball of the foot is in the stirrup, with the heels slightly lower than the toes. From the side, a straight line joins the rider's ear, shoulder, hip and heel. Another line runs from the horse's mouth to the rider's hand and elbow.

It takes a while to get used to moving your body with the movements of the horse. At first you are bound to feel stiff and awkward. At this stage, most beginners feel rather insecure in the saddle. This is why it is important to have a quiet, obedient horse.

The instructor will teach you how to control your mount using the aids. Your legs, seat, hands, voice and stick give signals to the horse, telling it to stop, start, turn, speed up or slow down. Each horse and each rider are different, but these basic signals are the same whether you are a complete novice or an international show-jumping star.

At a walk, the pony puts down each foot separately. You can count 1-2-3-4 as each hoof hits the ground. It is important that horses and ponies learn to step out smartly at the walk. There is nothing worse than a pony that is allowed to slouch along!

At the trot, the pony puts down its feet in diagonally opposite pairs. You can count 1-2, 1-2, as each pair of hooves hits the ground. The trot is a bouncier pace than the walk and it takes time to get used to it. Horses and ponies can trot fast or slow, with long steps or short. As you become more experienced, you will learn how to ask for the different types of trot.

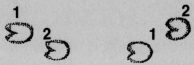

Getting Better with Practice

Lessons usually take place in groups of up to eight riders who have all reached roughly the same stage. Larger groups are not so useful as the instructor cannot give enough attention to each rider. With practice, the rider becomes more secure in the saddle.

Once the walk and trot have been mastered, the next pace to learn is the canter. During each canter stride, there is a period when the horse has all four feet off the ground, so the canter is quite a bouncy pace. However, most beginners find their first canter much smoother than their first attempts at trot. It is very easy to lose your balance during these early stages and slip off. As the pace is usually slow, you are unlikely to hurt yourself. Remember that all riders fall off from time to time.

Simple exercises in the saddle are useful for both rider and pony. They improve the rider's balance and strengthen muscles. They also teach the rider to move different parts of the body independently. At the same time, the pony gets used to unexpected movements on its back. It is important not to kick the pony in the ribs when leaning forward, as this would encourage it to trot on.

Lessons on the lunge are helpful from time to time. The pony is controlled from the ground by the instructor. This means that the rider can think about sitting in the correct position in the saddle. Exercises can be performed very safely on the lunge because there is less danger of the pony increasing speed or changing direction.

Left and Centre: This group of young riders are going 'round the world'. By swinging their legs over the front of the saddle, and then over the pony's back, they end up facing the pony's tail. Exercises like this give young riders confidence and improve their general balance. Of course, it is important that the ponies get used to these unusual activities gradually. A young or untrained pony could be very frightened by such strange movements and this could be dangerous for the rider.

Stretching up and then reaching down to touch the toes, first to the right and then to the left, increases suppleness. This exercise is performed first at halt. The next stage is to perform it at walk and even at trot. The difficulty is to keep control of the pony at the same time!

Learning to Jump

The rider must feel quite secure in the saddle before trying to jump. If a pony stops suddenly, it is very easy to slip over its head. For first lessons, the riding school must provide a pony that will jump willingly.

The rider's position for jumping is rather different from the position for riding on the flat. To help the pony, and to keep in balance, the rider must lean forward so that his or her weight comes slightly out of the saddle. The stirrups are also shortened slightly.

The first 'jump' is usually just a pole on the ground. The pace need not be any faster than a trot. Gradually, the pole is raised so that the rider gets the feeling of 'popping' over a small obstacle. Once a series of jumps is tried,

Left: It is important that beginners do not stop themselves falling back by hanging onto the reins. This is painful for the pony and stops it jumping properly. By letting go of the reins completely, this young rider is learning to keep her balance as she trots over a small jump.

Right: This is the first jump at canter. Notice how the rider is leaning forwards as the pony takes off.

Exercises are often performed using poles on the ground in front of a small jump. The poles are spaced so that the horse trots or canters over them and is then in the right place to take off.

the rider has to think about 'riding a course' as well as each individual jump.

There are different kinds of jumps. Show jumps consist of brightly painted poles, planks, gates etc. They can be built at different heights. If the pony hits a show jump, it will fall. Cross-country jumps are based on the natural obstacles that a horse might jump when out in the country – fallen trees, gates and hedges. They are natural in colour and do not fall if the pony hits them.

Many riding schools have riding clubs attached to them. They may also run small jumping competitions. These are great fun to enter if you can borrow a pony from the school. Learning at a riding school has its advantages. Riders get used to controlling different kinds of animal. They also see whether they like the sport before incurring the expense of keeping their own pony.

Here you can see how a horse goes over a small jump. As it approaches, it lowers its head to see how big a jump it has to make. Going over the jump, it stretches out its back and neck.

Ceremonies

It is not very long since the cavalry were an important part of any fighting force. Cavalry fought in the First World War. Although there is much discussion about exactly when the last cavalry charge took place, it was probably as late as 1953. Today the cavalry has been outdated by modern technology. Only a few countries still maintain small sections to give dignity and splendour to ceremonial occasions. Watching a group of these horses, most people feel stirred and excited. Perhaps it is because we know that horses have carried their warrior riders so bravely in the past.

Ceremonial horses are carefully matched in size and colour. Teams of black horses are usually used for funerals, lighter colours for happier occasions such as state weddings and coronations. Decked in their traditional finery, they make a splendid sight.

Above: These matching dapple grey horses are ridden by the Louis XVI guards of Versailles, France. Horses like these must be impeccably behaved, yet still show spirit and 'presence'.

Right: In complete contrast, but impressive in their own right, are the Senegalese Red Cavalry of Dakar, West Africa. The horses are of Oriental type, slight, but tough and wiry.

Behind the Scenes

A great deal of time, money and hard work go into looking after horses properly. In the wild, horses live outside, eating grass when they are hungry. Working horses have to be kept in stables if they are to be fit and healthy. They have to be regularly exercised, groomed, and fed concentrated high-protein food for the extra energy they need to work.

In a busy yard, the day begins early with the first feed. The stables are mucked out and the yard swept and tidied before the grooms can go for their breakfast. The horses are then exercised or have their training sessions. They are usually groomed before the lunchtime feed. In the afternoon, there may be more grooming, tack-cleaning, and tidying up. A hundred and one other jobs, from tending sick horses, mending fences, to just scrubbing out feed-buckets all have to be fitted in somewhere. At last the final feed is given and haynets and water-buckets are refilled for the night.

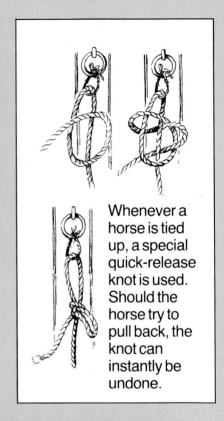

Whenever a horse is tied up, a special quick-release knot is used. Should the horse try to pull back, the knot can instantly be undone.

Right: The routine of the stable yard goes on day in and day out. There is no let-up even for Christmas! One of the first jobs of the day is mucking out. Using shovel and barrow, the soiled parts of the straw bed are removed. The remainder of the straw is spread out to dry. Getting rid of the used straw can be a problem. Most yards have a rich, fermenting muck heap. This rots down into manure. At intervals it is cleared out by mushroom-growers or by eager gardeners.

Left: The blacksmith, or farrier, makes regular visits. Horses have to work on roads and gravel surfaces. Their hooves must be protected otherwise they would soon wear away. Horse shoes are made of iron and nailed to the hoof. This farrier is using the hot-shoeing method. By heating up the iron, hammering and bending it, fine adjustments can be made so that the shoe fits perfectly. A badly-fitting shoe can cause the horse to go lame.

Left: Once the bed has been mucked out, new straw is added to make a deep, warm layer. The straw is banked up round the edges of the loose box to keep out the draughts. Some horses even use this bank as a pillow! If horses are allergic to straw, they have to be bedded down on wood shavings, sawdust, peat or shredded newspaper. In hot countries, even sand is sometimes used.

The Saddle and Bridle

It is vital that a saddle should fit properly. If it is too big or too small it will pinch or rub, causing sores. Even putting on a saddle carelessly can damage a horse's back, so that it is off work for weeks!

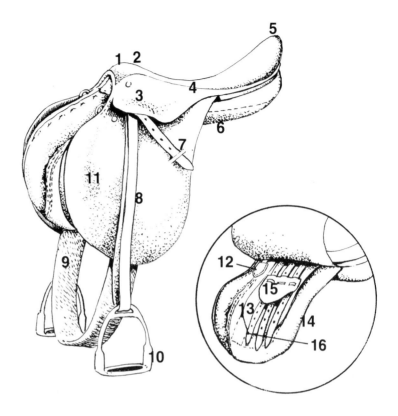

Key
1 Pommel
2 Waist
3 Skirt
4 Seat
5 Cantle
6 Lining
7 Surcingle loop
8 Stirrup leather
9 Girth
10 Stirrup iron
11 Saddle flap
12 Point pocket
13 Sweat flap
14 Panel
15 Buckle guard
16 Girth straps

A good riding school will teach the basics of pony care as well as how to ride. When tacking up, the saddle is put on first. The girth is undone on the left side and the stirrups run up. The saddle is placed forward of the pony's withers and gently slid back into position. The rider then checks on both sides that the flaps and girths are lying correctly.

The rider reaches down under the pony for the girth. This is done up tightly enough to stop the saddle slipping. There should still be two or three holes below the buckle.

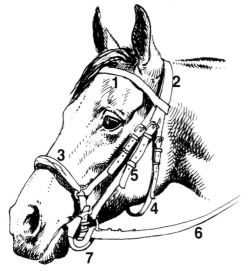

There are many different kinds of bridle to suit different horses and styles of riding. All can be adjusted and must fit properly for the horse to be comfortable. The one shown here is a plain snaffle bridle. It is a design that most riders meet very early in their riding careers.

1 **Browband**
2 **Headpiece**
3 **Noseband**
4 **Throatlash**
5 **Cheekpiece**
6 **Rein**
7 **Snaffle bit**

1

2

3

1. When the bridle is put on, the buckles of the noseband and throatlash are first undone. The reins are then placed over the pony's head and neck. The rider holds the headpiece in the right hand, level with the pony's ears. The bit rests in the left hand, level with the muzzle. The rider carefully feels with the fingers between the pony's lips for a gap in its teeth. This makes the pony open its mouth. At this point, the bit can be slipped in.
2. The headpiece is slipped gently over the pony's ears. The forelock and mane are smoothed out so that they lie flat.
3. The buckles of the throatlatch and noseband are done up. The throatlatch should be loose enough to allow a hand between it and the jaw. A cavesson noseband should allow two fingers between it and the front of the pony's face. Finally, the rider checks that all is straight from the front.

Grooming

Stabled horses and ponies have to be groomed every day. This is not simply to make their coats shine. Grooming keeps the skin clean and healthy. It stimulates the blood circulation and helps to tone up muscles under the skin. Grooming a pony involves hard work and elbow grease, and takes between half and three-quarters of an hour to do properly. Most horses and ponies seem to enjoy being groomed.

Horses and ponies living out in a field lead a much more natural life than stabled animals. Their coats develop a layer of grease which keeps them waterproof. Thorough grooming would remove this natural mackintosh and therefore should not be done. However, field ponies need to be checked over every day.

Each foot in turn is picked out using a hoof pick. This removes mud and stones. The feet are always picked out when the horse is groomed, and before it goes out to exercise.

A dandy brush is used to remove any loose dirt and mud. The dandy brush has stiff bristles. It is best not to use it on a pony which has been clipped or tends to be ticklish.

The body brush has denser, softer bristles. It is used with rhythmic, circular sweeps to remove dirt and scurf right down to the roots of the hair. It is cleaned from time to time with the curry comb.

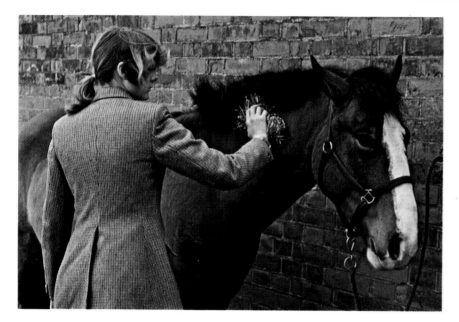

Wisping is a form of massage. The wisp is used quite forcefully on the muscular parts of the body. It tones up the muscles and improves the circulation. The wisp is never used on the bony parts of the body, such as the legs and ribs. Wisping, or strapping as it is called, is a very important part of grooming.

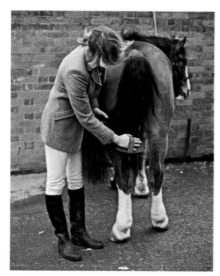

Far Left: With two separate sponges, the eyes and dock are cleaned. Care must be taken when handling the head. Sudden movements can make a pony 'head shy'.

Left: The tail is brushed out, a few strands at a time, starting at the bottom. The body brush is used because it is soft and will not break the hair. The groom stands slightly to one side, where she is less likely to be kicked.

By now the pony's coat should be gleaming! The mane is 'laid'. This means that it is dampened using a water brush. It is then brushed so that it hangs neatly on the right side of the neck. The hooves may then be brushed with hoof oil. The final touch is to remove any specks of dust with a folded stable-rubber. This thorough grooming routine is usually carried out after exercise, when the pores in the skin are open.

Travelling, Bandaging and Plaiting

Most horses and ponies have to get used to being driven from place to place. They may travel to shows every week, or they may only go in a horse-box or trailer when they are sold to a new owner. A pony that is not used to travelling quietly is a great nuisance.

The driver of the horse-box must brake and take corners smoothly. Even so, the pony has to learn to keep its balance and may be thrown around. If you look at a horse or pony coming out of a horse box, you will see that it is well-protected from bumps and bruises. There are boots and bandages on legs and tail. Even the top of the head, or poll, is padded. A frightened horse can sometimes throw its head up and receive a nasty injury on a low entrance or roof.

For shows and rallies, the entrants are turned out looking

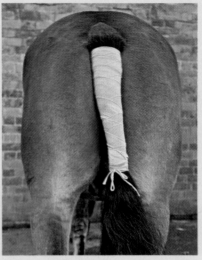

Some ponies lean on the back of the horse box. A tail bandage protects the tail from being rubbed raw.

1. The mane must be pulled before it can be plaited. It is then brushed and dampened.

2. Check the spacing between plaits. There should be an odd number plus the forelock.

3. Divide the lock of hair into three strands and plait tightly but evenly.

4. Take a needle and double thread. Wind it round the end of the plait. Secure with a knot.

5. Now, double the plait under in half, and then in half again to make a knob.

6. Wind the thread round the plait close to the base several times. Stitch to secure.

their best. The tack is cleaned and the pony groomed until it shines. The finishing touches are the plaiting of mane and tail. As well as looking smart, plaiting keeps the mane and tail tidy and out of the way during jumping competitions. Before it can be plaited, the mane has to be pulled, or thinned out, and shortened. Of course, ponies that live in a field do not have their manes pulled. They need their long hair to keep off the cold in winter and the flies in summer. Instead of plaiting, the tail can be pulled to lie neatly.

A good riding school will teach you the basics of how to look after a pony, as well as how to ride it. There are also courses and tests in stable management. It takes expertise and practice to turn out a horse the picture of health and smart in every detail. That is why it is important to think carefully about the time, knowledge and expense involved before going out to buy a pony for the first time.

Below: This pony is fully dressed for a journey. Special boots cover the hocks and knees in case of a fall. If you look carefully, you will see that the lower straps of the knee boots have been done up too tightly. The pony will have difficulty bending its knees when it tries to walk up the ramp into the box. The lower legs are protected by thick padded bandages. The headpiece of the headcollar is also padded. Finally a rug, held in place by a surcingle, keeps the pony warm in cold weather.

A Job with Horses

The jobs that come to mind most readily are always the most glamorous. Sadly, the number of people who make a living out of jumping winning rounds at the Horse of the Year Show are very few. The majority of people who work with horses are concerned with their routine care. A horse is often kept for 22 out of 24 hours in a small stable, so its every need has to be attended to. This is the job of the groom.

The hours a groom works are long and he or she has to start very early in the morning. There is not as much time off as in an office job, and the pay is low. But for anyone who enjoys the outdoors and wants to work with horses, it is a tremendously rewarding job. It is important to get some kind of qualification, either before you start, or while you are working. There are exams set at various grades in horse

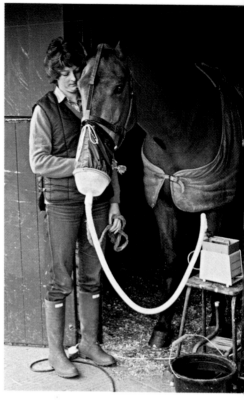

Above: Caring for sick horses is a specialized branch of veterinary science. This fine hunter has a problem with its wind. When fitted with this special mask, the horse breathes in a drug that helps to clear its lungs.

Left: Saddles are still made by hand in many cases, using the traditional materials of leather and wood. They are often made to fit a particular horse's back, just like a hand-made shoe. A good saddle costs hundreds of pounds but, if properly looked after, it will last a lifetime.

Right: The mounted police are called in to control crowds. Few people will stand and argue with a large and imposing horse! Police horses are rigorously trained not to flinch or shy, whatever the noise level.

mastership. Many riding schools and technical colleges run courses in preparation for these tests.

Another popular job is to work as an instructor in a riding school. It is advisable to hold a recognized qualification. The minimum qualification in Britain is the Assistant Instructor's Certificate, and there are courses at riding schools and technical colleges. When applying to a riding school, it is vital to find out the terms and conditions of the course. Some establishments expect students to work in the yard in return for food, lodging and instruction. This gives good practical experience but it is important to work out the details before you start. You should always discuss how many hours you will be expected to work, how much instruction you will be given and how long the course of training will last. In other cases, riding schools and training establishments offer courses which are paid for by the students or their parents. Usually these courses are more intensive and shorter.

Above: A groom checks that all the tack is present and correct at the Badminton horse trials. A piece of worn stitching could cause an accident.

Vets often specialize in the care of horses. To be a vet, you have to study hard. For example, you need at least three 'A' levels in science subjects to get into one of the seven veterinary colleges in Britain. As an animal auxiliary nurse, you act as an assistant to a vet. For this you need 'O' levels, including science and maths, to be accepted for a two-year course at a polytechnic.

To train as a farrier, it is now possible to do a course at a technical college. Study involves the anatomy of the horse as well as the practical side of this craft. Otherwise, youngsters go on an apprenticeship with an experienced farrier. In the past, the village blacksmith worked from his smithy doing all kinds of ironwork, including shoeing horses. Today, it is more likely that the farrier will have a portable electric forge which he takes on his rounds.

Farriery is a job that few girls train for because it is such hard physical work. In making saddlery, however, dexterity and patience are more important. Being apprenticed to an experienced saddler is the usual way to learn. Terms and payment should be agreed beforehand.

Left: The shoe is fitted to the horny outside edge of the foot so that the horse feels no pain. The farrier may adjust the fit of a ready-made shoe, or he may make the shoe himself from a straight bar of iron. Here, the farrier is checking that the shoe fits perfectly while still hot.

Working in a racing yard is an extremely responsible job, for the horses are often very valuable indeed. For this reason the work is usually higher paid, but standards are also very high. Grooms have two or three horses in their care and may ride them out at exercise. In races, experienced jockeys are employed. This job is highly prized, but there are no special training courses to go on that will qualify you as a jockey!

Above: Racehorses are often ridden out at exercise by their grooms. Here, Red Rum, who won the Grand National three times, is exercised along the sands at Southport. If you have ever tried running through sand, you will understand how good it is for building muscle!

The Spanish Riding School

There have been fashions in riding just as there are in most things. In the 16th and 17th centuries, a great deal of study went into working out the best ways of training horses. A number of centres were founded, including the famous Spanish Riding School in Vienna.

The horses used are Spanish Lipizzaners, specially bred for the purpose. They are trained to be very 'collected'. This means that, instead of being allowed to move with a naturally long, low outline, they are encouraged to 'shorten'. The quarters have to work more energetically so that they come under the horse, and the head and neck are raised and flexed.

Below: This horse was trained in Vienna. It was sold and now lives in Australia. It takes part in spectacular displays which are based on the work of the Spanish Riding School.

The Spanish Riding School horses are trained over a period of several years. Like athletes, they specialize in certain movements, depending on their own natural ability. The most famous of these movements are the 'airs above the ground'. Some are performed with a rider. In others, the horse is controlled by a rider standing on the ground. In the *capriole*, the horse leaps high in the air at the same time kicking out behind. In the *levade* the horse stands on its hind legs with its rider still in position.

In the capriole, the horse leaps in the air, at the same time kicking out with its hind legs. This photograph was taken at a recent performance of the Spanish Riding School at Wembley, London.

Riding Western

If any country can be said to have a tradition of horsemanship, it must be the United States of America. But in fact the history of the horse in America is quite short. The wild horse died out in America in prehistoric times. It was not until adventurers from Europe found their way to the New World that horses were reintroduced.

In 1493, Christopher Columbus visited Haiti in the West Indies. He took 30 horses with him. When the Spanish Conquistadores set sail in search of gold and territory, they also had horses on board. In time, some of these animals were lost, traded or stolen. Some fell into the hands of the native tribes of Indians. With poor feeding and random breeding, these horses gave rise to herds of ponies which were tough and wiry. Although the Indians had never seen horses before, they soon proved to be natural riders. They rode with no saddle or stirrups, but they could shoot a bow

Above: On their agile ponies, the Indians hunted the buffalo. They used every part of the animal for food, clothing and shelter. The cowboys found that the buffalo competed with their cattle for grazing. In just a few years, they wiped out the entire species.

Left: Steer-roping is a popular rodeo sport. It grew out of the day-to-day work of the cowboys who tended vast herds of cattle in the Wild West. This painting is by Charles M. Russell.

and arrow at a gallop. They shielded themselves from the bullets of the newcomers by sliding down and hiding behind the flanks of their mounts as they went.

Whenever ships set sail from the Old World for the Americas, there were always a number of horses on board. These first imports had to be very tough. The voyage across the Atlantic took three months and the horses were tied up on deck, often with no shelter or exercise. Not surprisingly, half of them died. On arrival, the ones that survived were quickly put to work. They were the only means of transport across unexplored country. They helped to clear the land that the new settlers had to farm in order to live.

The tradition of the cowboy grew out of cattle-ranching. Cattle raised on the plains of central and western America were driven in their thousands to the railway towns and markets of the east. The cowboys often spent months on horseback during these massive drives. Their horses had great stamina and a natural 'cow sense' – they knew which way a wandering steer would dodge even before it moved.

Competition grew up between the men as to who was the best roper or bronco-rider. Contests were held to prove it. These contests became more formal and were organized into 'rodeos', the Spanish name for a round-up. The cattle drives and round-ups of the old West have long since ceased, but rodeo sports still attract huge audiences.

The five most important events of the rodeo are calf-roping, steer-wrestling, saddle bronc-riding, bareback bronc-riding and bull-riding. In calf-roping, the rider has to lassoo the animal and tie its legs together as if it were ready for branding. The rider who does this in the fastest time wins. Horses for this event are trained to stop as soon as the rider jumps off. The end of the lassoo is attached to the front of the saddle, and the horse keeps the rope taut so that the calf cannot escape. In steer-wrestling, the cowboy rides full pelt alongside a long-horned bull. He dives at the horns and twists the animal onto its side. Another rider gallops close to the other side of the bull to prevent it veering away.

Right: Horses that compete in steer-roping competitions must be extremely quick on their feet, and able to turn and stop sharply. As they gallop along, they are usually watching the quarry as eagerly as their rider. Once the lassoo is in place, it is the horse that keeps the rope taut, while the rider vaults off to tie the steer's legs together.

Below: In bronco-riding, extra points are awarded for horses that buck the most wildly. This is why competitors are eager to ride the most difficult horses. This photograph shows the Texas Prison Rodeo.

Bronco-riding is the classic rodeo sport. Marks are given for the horse that bucks the most wildly as well as for the rider who manages to stay on board the longest. The time limit is eight seconds in bareback, and ten seconds in the saddle bronc class. The horses are usually kept specially for bronco competitions. They cannot be ridden normally and

are made to buck by having a bucking strap fastened tightly round their flanks behind the saddle.

At the larger rodeos there are other contests which test the skills of horse and rider. They include chariot-racing for single horses, and chuck-wagon racing, in which teams of horses compete.

Below: Chariot-racing drew vast crowds in the days of ancient Rome. A modern version takes place at the Calgary Stampede, one of the biggest rodeos in Canada.

Barrel-racing involves galloping in and out of a triangular course of barrels. The fastest time wins. It is really the Western version of 'bending' races. It demands speed and agility, and is the one rodeo sport in which women take part.

As well as rodeo sports, the Western style of riding may be used in long-distance and endurance rides. These are also becoming very popular in Europe. The course is mapped out beforehand and may be a hundred kilometres or more in length. It covers a variety of terrain and there are regular check-points along the way. It is not simply a question of the fastest time winning. The horses are awarded points for physical condition, and close checks are made on pulse and respiration rates.

The traditional Western stock saddle and bridle are very different from the light, flat saddle used for most types of

Above: These riders are herding sheep in Utah, USA. In some places where there are no roads, horses are still used to check livestock. Landrovers or other motor vehicles are expensive to run and do not always stand up well to the rough terrain.

riding in Europe. The saddle has its origins in the style of saddle used by the warriors of medieval times. The pommel and cantle are high. This gives the rider more support, and can be more comfortable for many hours in the saddle. The high pommel is designed so that it can be used as a hitching-post for the lariat. There are tie-points on the saddle for attaching food, water, spare clothing and anything else the cowboy needs for his day's work.

In Western-style riding, the rider has a much straighter leg position, and does not rise to the trot. For long distances, a slow, loping canter is the preferred pace. Though the Western saddle is comfortable, it is too restricting to be used for jumping, apart from the odd log or ditch. Western horses are also taught to 'neck-rein'. Simply pressing the rein against the side of the neck makes the animal turn instantly. There is the lightest possible contact with the horse's mouth.

This Western-style bridle does not have a noseband. The reins are attached to long 'cheeks'. These give greater leverage on the bit and can cause the horse pain in the hands of a careless rider.

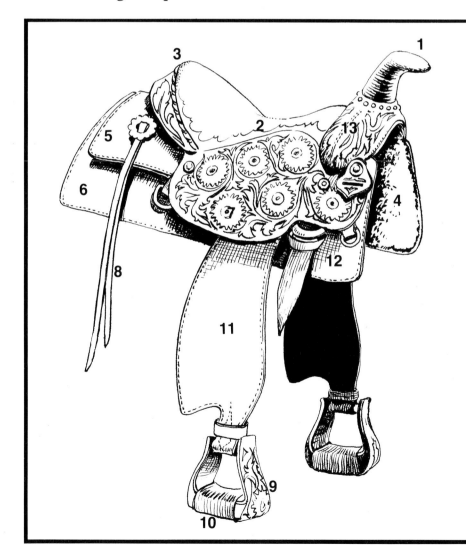

The Western stock saddle is larger and heavier than the European hunter saddle. It is designed to spread the weight of both saddle and rider evenly over a large area of the horse's back. This is very useful when a horse has to be ridden for several hours over long distances, as it cuts down the risk of saddle sores.

Key
1 Horn
2 Seat
3 Cantle
4 Woolskin lining
5 Back jockey
6 Skirt
7 Side jockey
8 Saddle strings
9 Stirrup
10 Tread cover
11 Fender
12 Front jockey
13 Fork

Horses in Entertainment

Horses have played a part in all aspects of our lives. As well as transporting us, fetching and carrying for us, tilling our fields and even fighting for us, they also give us fun, sport and entertainment. One of the highlights of a trip to the circus must be seeing the dazzlingly decorated liberty horses go through their paces. No procession or festival is complete without horses to add a touch of the dramatic.

Wherever there are horses, sports and games are played to prove the skill of mount or rider. The tournaments of the Middle Ages were a chance to practise the techniques of wartime. They were also a popular spectator sport. There were some safety measures – swords and spears were blunted, and there were rules forbidding striking below the belt. It was considered unsporting to wound an opponent's

Below: Jousting today is not as dangerous as the medieval version. Troupes of actors dress up in the costume of knights of old, though without the heavy armour. The ends of the lances are blunted, and the knights wear padded clothing. They make an impressive scene, performing on the lawns in front of a stately home or castle.

horse. However, the contestants would still manage to damage each other fairly seriously. The aim of jousting was to unseat the opponent using a long spear. Other contests included striking a target, or picking up a lady's 'favour' at a full gallop.

There were rich rewards of gold for the winners. Troups of professional performers wandered round the country from tournament to tournament. These 'knights errant' were able to make quite a good living out of their winnings. Today, throughout the summer season, tournaments are re-enacted at stately homes and castles.

Police horses are trained to be absolutely obedient. They must stand quietly in noisy traffic, football crowds and even riots if necessary. As a change from their routine work, they also take part in displays and competitions. Most animals are afraid of fire and in the wild always run away from it. This horse shows its high standard of training, and complete trust in its rider, by jumping through flaming hoops.

For some people, watching is not enough. In Britain, there are organizations which stage large-scale mock battles. These may last a whole weekend, with hundreds of infantry, cavalry, officers and supporters camping out ready to re-enact a battle from the Civil War or some other period of history. Everyone takes great pride in getting the details of costumes and events exactly right. The horses are expected to charge realistically even though they may never have heard the sounds of cannon and gunfire before.

In films and television, horses add drama and realism. Gunfights between cowboys and Indians would be less exciting without the stunt riders and their mounts who throw themselves to the ground at pre-arranged signals. The horses are trained to specialize in certain movements, whether it is throwing themselves over backwards, rearing or just dropping to the ground. Once trained, the horses will perform these feats over and over again.

Right: Armed to the teeth, this ceremonial archer is taking part in the Meiji Festival near Tokyo in Japan.

Below: The world of cowboys and Indians is long past, but the old stories of gunfights and survival against all the odds are powerful. Here the atmosphere of the Wild West is recreated on film.

Famous Horses

Some very famous horses belong to legends and stories. You may have heard of the winged horse, Pegasus, or the half-horse, half-human centaurs of the ancient Greeks. Horses have also taken leading roles in novels and films. For example, the story of Black Beauty is about a London carriage horse, fallen on hard times. The book was written by Anna Sewell, an invalid who relied on a pony and trap to get around. There are also the genuine stars of the horse world – horses whose efforts have saved lives, carried vital news, or been outstanding in sporting events.

Right: Dick Turpin was the most infamous highwayman of all times. As a young man, he led a gang of robbers, attacking travellers on the road between London and Oxford. In Whitechapel, London, he accidentally shot his companion. The story goes that he escaped the law by riding all the way to York on his faithful horse Black Bess. He was finally hanged for horse-stealing in 1793.

Left: Paul Revere's famous ride is one of the best-loved stories of American history. Revere fought against the British for the independence of his country. On 18 April 1775, he learned that the British planned to sieze American arms stored at Concorde, Massachusetts. On a borrowed horse, Paul Revere rode at great speed through the night, to warn as many people as possible what was going to happen. As a result, when the British arrived the next day, there were armed men waiting for them.

Right: The Grand National is unique, perhaps the greatest of all horse races. The course is long, about 4½ miles. Many say that the 30 enormous fences are the toughest of any race. Apart from their great height and width, they are built up with thorn, rather than the usual birch and spruce. Very few of the many starters manage to complete the course. The great Red Rum is the only horse to have won the National three times. What is more he came second twice.

The Competition Horse

Many top international riders began their competitive careers in gymkhana games. Doing the sack race or vaulting on a pony bareback may not seem to have much in common with top-class show-jumping. However, they do teach horse and rider how to work together. Riders gain confidence and balance, and also have a good deal of fun.

The Pony Club was started to improve the horsemanship of its members. At a Pony Club rally, games are always included after the hard work is over. A good gymkhana pony must respond instantly to its rider's aids to stop, start and turn. It must be fast, but unafraid of noisy supporters or strange pieces of equipment. Many a pony that refused to jump, or was not handsome enough for show classes, has proved to be excellent at the egg-and-spoon race!

Right: In Britain, Pony Club teams compete every year for the Prince Philip Cup. The finals are held at the Horse of the Year Show, and it is a great thrill to be a member of one of the six winning teams. There are relay races, apple-bobbing races, musical chairs, potato-picking, flag races, paper races and many more.

Below: In the stepping-stone race, it is not just the footwork of the rider that counts. The pony must learn to trot willingly beside its rider, however fast or slowly he is going.

Left: Even the smallest and least experienced rider can take part in something. Leading-rein races and even leading-rein jumping are always popular. The winner needs to have a fit parent as well as a willing pony!

Show-Jumping

Show-jumping is fast growing in popularity. Today, large indoor arenas have been built, so the sport can take place all the year round. Spectators sit in comfort, listening to an informed commentary, and with a good view of everything that happens. Now that the major competitions are televised, top international riders and their horses have become household names. The horses reach their peak at about ten years old, and have only a few years at the top. The best riders, however, can look forward to longer careers!

At the highest levels, competitors travel widely all over Europe and America. Among the most famous show-jumping arenas are at Aachen in Germany, Rome, Madrid, Rotterdam, Toronto, Dublin, Hickstead and Wembley.

Right: The German rider Hasse Hoffmann on Parco at Rotterdam in 1980. The concentration and determination necessary to win really show on this rider's face.

Below: David Broome has had a long and successful career in show-jumping, as an amateur and professional. He has ridden for Britain many times, winning a World Championship and two bronze Olympic medals. Here he rides Queensway Philco at Calgary in 1981.

The costs of show-jumping are very high. Travelling by air is faster and smoother for the horses than by sea and road, but also more expensive. Untrained and unproven horses with promise can cost enormous sums of money to buy. Successful show-jumpers are worth even more! But the popularity of show-jumping has also attracted people into backing it. Commercial organizations may sponsor riders and their teams of horses. For some, this is the only way to continue in their chosen fields. In return, the sponsors are happy if they get publicity in the media.

To compete successfully at the highest levels, riders must devote their lives to show-jumping. Many have turned professional. For them, the World Championships are more important than the Olympic Games, which are only open to amateur riders.

Below: The Americans have a distinct and fluid style of show-jumping. Melanie Smith takes Calypso over a wide spread.

Left: Malcolm Pyrah with his outstanding horse, Towerlands Anglezarke, jumping in an indoor arena. There is usually less space available indoors. Horses have to jump neatly and turn sharply.

Right: The Olympic Games are held every four years, at a different venue. It is a great honour to be chosen as a member of the team. Here, Alwin Schockemöhle jumps Warwick Rex in the 1976 Games at Montreal, winning a gold medal.

Most show-jumpers begin their careers riding ponies at small local shows for fun. Gradually, if they have talent and determination, they may progress to county and national level. From the smallest to the largest show, classes are graded. This ensures that horses of similar standard jump against each other. Both horse and rider learn over a number of years by practice and experience. The top show-jumpers save their best horses for the biggest competitions. However, most of them also have a string of young horses in training. From these will come the prize-winners of the future. They must be given experience by competing in the many small shows that never appear on television.

Dressage

To an outsider, dressage is the least spectacular of all the equestrian sports. For one thing, it is the least cut and dried. It is not simply a case of who can jump the highest or go the fastest. Dressage is all about style, and it is the way the horse and rider perform that matter.

Dressage training aims to improve the natural paces of the horse by a series of exercises. A trained horse is supple, light, obedient and elegant to watch. In a dressage contest, each horse performs the same series of movements. Marks out of ten are awarded for each movement. There are different levels of test, from the Basic Training level up to Olympic standard. Every competition horse does some dressage training. Show-jumpers, for example, need the suppleness and balance they gain through their work on the flat in order to jump with speed and accuracy.

Above: Dressage on the Continent of Europe is generally better than in Britain or the United States. The Germans are particularly good at it. The heavier-built, German-bred horses tend to be more suited to dressage training than English Thoroughbreds. This is Swiss rider Ulrich Lehmann competing on Widin in 1980.

Left: Jennie Loriston-Clarke is Britain's most successful competition dressage rider. On her most advanced horse, Dutch Courage, she won a bronze medal in the 1978 World Championships. Here she competes with Dutch Courage at Goodwood in 1981.

Dressage exercises are rather like gymnastics for the horse. It has to learn to use its muscles in quite a new way. Exercises encourage the horse to bend its back, so that it can go round a corner in a smooth, balanced curve.

Above: In lateral work, the horse moves sideways. This illustration shows a half pass to the right. The horse moves to the right, bending in the direction in which it is going.

Above: The pirouette is an advanced movement and needs a high level of training. The horse moves in a small circle, pivoting on its hind legs. It may be done at walk or canter.

Below: Within the ordinary paces of walk, trot and canter, the horse can be taught to make fine adjustments. It can be trained to go with long steps or short, still keeping the same speed.

On the right below is an extended trot. As its name suggests, the horse covers a lot of ground, and its whole outline is stretched out.

On the left below is a collected trot. The horse takes shorter but active steps. Its centre of gravity is also rather further back.

Eventing

Eventing is the most thrilling and exciting of the equestrian sports. It began in Europe as a military competition, to test cavalry horses. This is why endurance and courage play such an important part in it. Eventing used to be called combined training. The reasons are obvious – the test includes dressage, steeplechasing, galloping fast across country over fixed obstacles, and show-jumping. At the highest level there are the three-day events. Below this are two-day and one-day events, all graded in difficulty.

The first day of a three-day event is devoted to dressage. The standard is not as high as in a pure dressage competition, but this is not surprising. The horses are fighting fit, ready for the hard work to come. It is very difficult to persuade such a horse to perform a calm, accurate test.

The second day is the high point of the event, the speed and endurance section. Instead of the top hats and tails worn for dressage, competitors put on sweaters, crash helmets and stop-watches. There are four phases – several kilometres of roads and tracks; a steeplechase course; more

Left: Mark Phillips has been extremely successful in three-day eventing, winning Badminton on four occasions. Here he rides Persian Holiday in the dressage stage of the Burghley three-day event.

roads and tracks and finally the cross-country. In this phase, the horses gallop over 30 to 35 obstacles set in undulating countryside. This is the phase that attracts most attention from the public. From the ground the jumps look enormous. Course-builders use their imagination to construct drop fences, banks, walls, often set in awkward combinations, and of course the famous water-jumps. Each phase has to be completed in an optimum time, though extra points are not awarded for beating this time. Penalty points are given for time faults. A refusal costs 20 points and a fall 60. These scores are added to the dressage score.

Above: French rider S. Bruneau jumps boldly into the Badminton lake on Velox D'Escla. It is all too easy for the horse to lose its balance as it hits the water.

Left: Eventing is not as widespread in the United States as in Europe, but there are some very good American riders. They include Bruce Davidson who has twice won the World Championships. This is Sandy Pflueger with Free Scot.

On the final day, the horses are inspected by the official vet to make sure that they are still fit and sound – because the cross-country phase puts a very severe strain on them. Finally, there is the show-jumping competition. The horses must prove that they can jump fluently and well, despite their efforts on the previous day. For extra spectator interest, the competitors jump in reverse order.

A number of three-day events are held in Europe and the United States. Perhaps the most famous of all is held at Badminton on the estate of the Duke of Beaufort. On cross-country day, more people watch than at a cup final.

Left: The morning after cross-country day can be nerve-wracking. If the horse does not pass its veterinary inspection, all the work and preparation of the previous weeks are wasted. Here a horse's legs are hosed down to soothe any possible swelling.

Right: From galloping over the cross-country fences, the horses have to change their style of jumping completely. Show-jumping needs a slower and more accurate approach. Here, Sue Benson demonstrates on Monocle at Locko in 1981.

Long-distance Riding

Long-distance riding is very popular in the United States and Australia, and has a growing following in Europe. There are different branches of the sport. In trail-riding, groups of riders get together to follow a route, perhaps for five or six days. This is done purely for fun, but it may start an interest in competitive long-distance riding. Competition courses are planned out beforehand and cover a variety of countryside. The distance may be a hundred kilometres or more, and has to be completed within certain time limits. The pace usually averages out at a steady trot. As well as timing, the fitness of the horse is taken into account. At various points, the heart rate, respiration, and the time they take to return to normal are checked. Many different types of horse can take part in long-distance riding. The competitor feels a great sense of achievement if he or she manages to bring home a fit horse within the time allowed.

Right: Long-distance riding grew out of trail-riding which is done just for fun. Here, a couple enjoy a ride out into the countryside of Australia.

Below: Like marathon runners, long-distance horses have to go into training weeks beforehand. So that the horses are not over-stressed, there is often a minimum as well as a maximum time limit.

Driving

Horse-drawn transport has long gone out of date, but driving is becoming popular as a sport. Would-be drivers, or whips as they are known, start by learning to control a single horse. The vehicles are of traditional shape. Some are real antiques but many are now purpose-built. There are governess carts, gigs, dog-carts, phaetons, landaus and many more. A governess cart is so named because it was used by the governess of a wealthy family. She would sit sideways, so that she could keep an eye on her charges while she was driving. A gig has forward-facing seats and two large wheels.

Above: George Bowman is famous for his skill in the driving world. He is putting his team of bays through their paces at the sand-pit obstacle in the British National Driving Championships.

It has to be balanced so all the weight does not rest on the shafts, which are supported by the horse.

Horses can be driven in different combinations. Two horses side by side are called a pair. One behind the other is a tandem. A unicorn consists of a pair of horses with a single horse in front. Perhaps most thrilling to watch are the teams of four-in-hand.

There are various branches of driving, all with their own types of competition. In showing classes, marks are given for the appearance of the whole turn-out. Scurries, or obstacle courses against the clock, are exciting for the audience. The course is set out between pairs of cones and through narrow gates, with plenty of tight turns. The smallest ponies are often the nippiest. Ride-and-drive competitions are for horses that can be both ridden and driven. Most riding horses can be broken to harness, especially if they are calm by nature and sensible in traffic.

Below: Combined driving competitions include a cross-country phase. The water obstacle is a good vantage-point for spectators.

In America, Australia and parts of Europe, though not so much in Britain, harness races are very popular. However, they are more likely to take place on a dirt track than on snow! The vehicles are stripped down to the bare minimum so that they are as light as possible.

Combined driving is the driving equivalent of a three-day event. At the beginning, marks are given for presentation. Every buckle and piece of harness must be polished until it gleams! The next section is a dressage test. Just like a ridden test, a series of exercises are performed, with marks given for each movement. Then, there is the marathon phase, which includes a cross-country course. There are specially-built

obstacles, including water to cross, steep slopes up and down, and difficult going such as sand or mud. Skilful driving is needed, for it is not unusual for a carriage to turn over if turns are too tight or too fast. Finally, there is the obstacle course. Within a time limit, the competitors have to get round a twisting course, through pairs of cones, without touching any of them.

Polo

The word 'polo' comes from the Tibetan word 'pulu' meaning a ball. Polo is a very ancient game. Versions of it have been played for centuries, and still are in different parts of the world. The present game evolved in India in the last century, where it was the sport of Indian princes and rulers. It was taken up by the British cavalry in India, and gradually came to the West.

To an outsider, polo looks a rough game with few rules. The players seem to be doing their best to damage each other! In fact, the rules are very strict. There are four players in each team, together with mounted umpires. The aim is to hit the ball into the opposite goal. In the meantime, 'riding off' can take place. One player forces his pony against his opponent's, pushing it off course. The game is played in a series of six or seven chukkas, each lasting 7½ minutes. Between chukkas the players change ponies, for the pace is very fast. Penalties are given if riders break the rules of right of way, bumping an opponent, or misusing their sticks.

Polo players learn the different ways of hitting the ball on a wooden horse in a polo pit. Once they have mastered the theory, they can put it into practice on a live animal. All

Polo is fast and can be dangerous. The sticks are swung at great speed. Players wear helmets and knee-guards. Their ponies' legs are protected by boots and bandages.

88

players must hold the stick in their right hand, which is a disadvantage if you happen to be left-handed. Experts say that it is easier to teach someone who is good at ball games how to ride well enough to play polo, than it is to teach a rider how to hit a ball. In polo there does not seem to be very much time for the niceties of riding.

The players ride ponies, not horses, though the ponies are usually about 15 hands high. The action of a pony is smoother than a horse, and this gives a more level platform from which to hit the ball. The ponies have to be fearless, and able to turn and stop instantly. They must be very fast but tough. Polo is played widely in Argentina, and the country exports some of the best polo ponies. They are Criollo, or ranch ponies, crossed with Thoroughbreds for greater height and speed.

In the Hunzakut in North-West Pakistan, the local people play a type of polo. The game is known as Bushkasi. In the past it had few rules. There was no formally marked-out pitch and, instead of a ball, the players used the head of a human enemy.

In the working hunter classes, marks are given for the way that competitors jump, as well as for looks. This pretty palomino is Exton Honeywood, the champion working hunter pony at the Shropshire and West Show in 1980.

Showing

Showing classes are the beauty contests of the horse world. When exhibitors search for next season's winners, they look for horses with good basic conformation and action. In other words, the animal must be well made, with limbs and body in proportion, and must have good basic paces. The art of showing is then to produce the animal looking its best on the day. It is attention to detail that counts – from the degree of polish on a hoof, to the precise angle of the saddle. As in human beauty contests, tricks of the trade are learned by experience. Putting many tiny plaits into a mane can draw attention to a well-carried neck. Special marks brushed onto the quarters will show off good muscle or shape.

There is a show class for every type of animal, for hunters, hacks, horses under saddle and horses led 'in-hand'. There are classes for mares with foals, stallions and also for particular breeds. Some classes are judged solely on manners, looks and action. In working show classes, competitors must also complete a course of jumps.

Left: A champion Welsh cob is trotted out in-hand, so that the judges can study the way it moves. This is just as important as the animal's looks.

Below: Showing has a strong following in America, Australia and Britain. It also has its supporters in Continental Europe. This particular show took place in Avenches, France.

Racing

Thoroughbreds are raced all over the world, although the rules differ from country to country. Flat race horses are put into training when they are very young. They are raced at two, and the classic flat race, the Epsom Derby, is for three-year-olds. Owners and trainers must be more patient with their jumpers, for they need to be more mature before they start. Racing over jumps, or steeplechasing, began in Ireland. It got its name because country gentlemen got together informally to race their horses across country over gates, ditches and hedges. They often took two church steeples as their starting and finishing points. Today the biggest steeplechasing course is probably the Grand National, except perhaps for the four-mile Gran Pardubice which is held in Czechoslovakia every October.

Left: Newmarket is the home of British horse-racing. There are racing stables on every corner. At certain times of the day, horses going out to exercise even have right of way over cars. Here a Newmarket trainer watches his string go through their paces.

Left: Horses that succeed over jumps need stamina and speed, as well as jumping ability. The courses are longer, and the horses are more mature than in flat racing. This race took place in Kentucky.

Right: Where horses race together there will be betting! The bookies keep in touch with each other by their own special form of sign language. This ensures that the odds offered on any horse do not vary much from one bookie to another.

Hurdling is the junior branch of racing over jumps. In Britain, hurdles are only 3 feet 6 inches, compared with the 4 feet 6 inches of steeplechasing. Good hurdlers gallop over them, hardly breaking their stride. Many horses learn to jump over hurdles, but winning hurdlers do not necessarily make good steeplechasers.

There is a great deal of money to be won and lost in horse-racing. Betting is a very important part of the sport. Many people who have never actually been on a racecourse are addicted to betting on the horses! Large sums of money can be won, especially in flat racing. Even when the winner has retired, owners and trainers are prepared to pay colossal stud fees in the hopes of finding their own Derby or Gold Cup winner.

Above: In flat races, the distances are short. To make sure that the horses all start together, starting-stalls are used. The horses are trained to spring out when the gates open.

Right: Racing is an exciting sport, and it can be a dangerous one. If one of the front horses in a tight group falls or swerves, it can easily bring down the horses behind.

Index

Aachen 72
Aids 34-5
American Saddlebred horse 22
Appaloosa horse 21, 22
Arab horse 12-13, 14, 22
Ardennes horse 18
Austrian Haflinger pony 25

Badminton 78, 79
Bandaging 48-9
Barb horse 22
Barrel-racing 62
Benson, Sue 81
Blacksmith 43, 52
Bowman, George 84
Breed societies 12-13
Breeding 11, 12-23, 24
Bridles 45, 63
British National Driving
  Championships 84
Bronco-riding 58-61
Broome, David 72
Bruneau, S. 78-9
Bull-riding 58
Bushkasi 88-9
Byerley, Captain 14
Byerley Turk 14

Calf-roping 58
Calgary stampede 60-1
Camargue horse 10-11
Canter 36, 38-9
Capriole 55
Cart-horse 13
Cattle-ranching 57
Centaurs 68
Ceremonies 40-1
Chariot-racing 60-1
Chuck-wagon racing 60-1
Clydesdale horse 18
Colour 20-1
Columbus, Christopher 56
Connemara pony 16
Cowboys 57, 66
Criollo pony 89
Cross-country riding 78-9, 81,
  85

Dales pony 16
Darley Arabian horse 14
Darley, Thomas 14
Dartmoor pony 16
Davidson, Bruce 81
Dismounting 33
Dressage 76-7, 78

Driving 84-7

Epsom Derby 92, 94
European Show-jumping
  Championships 5
Eventing 78-81
Exercises, for rider 30-39
Exmoor pony 16-17

Falabella pony 16-17
Farrier 43, 52
Feeding 32, 42
Fell pony 16
Fjord pony 17

Godolphin Arabian 14
Gran Pardubice 92
Grand National 53, 68, 92
Groom, being a 42-3, 46-7,
  50-1, 53
Grooming 42, 46-7, 50-1, 53
Gymkhana games 25, 70-1

Harness racing 86-7
Heavy horse 13, 18-19, 24-5
Highland ponies 16
Hoffmann, Hasse 72-3
Horse of the Year Show 50, 70
Hurdling 94

Jockeys 53
Jousting 64-5
Jumping 25, 38-9, 72-5, 78

Khan, Ghengis 28-9

Lehmann, Ulrich 76
Levade 55
Lippizaner horse 20
Long-distance riding 62, 82-3
Loriston-Clarke, Jennie 76
Lunging 34, 36

Markings 20-1
Mongols 28-9
Morgan horses 22
Morgan, Justin 22
Mounting 32

Neck-reining 63
New Forest pony 13, 16, 21

Olympic Games 72, 74-5, 76

Palomino horse 20-1, 90
Percheron horse 13, 21
Pflueger, Sandy 80-1
Phillips, Mark 78

Plaiting 48-9
Points 20
Polo 88-9
Ponies 9, 10, 13, 16-17, 20-1,
  24-5, 42, 48, 70, 88-9
Pony Club 70-1
Prehistoric horse 8-9
Przewalski, Colonel 9
Przewalski horse 8, 9
Pyrah, Malcolm 4-5, 74-5

Quick-release knot 44

Racing 14-15, 92-5
Red Rum 52-3, 68-9
Revere, Paul 68
Riding-schools 30, 39, 49, 51,
  54-5
Rodeos 58-62

Saddlebred horse 22
Saddles 44, 50, 63
Schockemohle, Alwin 75
Shetland pony 16-17, 21, 25
Shire horse 18-19
Show-jumping 25, 72-5, 78
Showing 90-1
Smith, Melanie 74
Spanish Lipizzaner horse 54
Spanish Riding School 54-5
Standardbred horse 22
Steeplechasing 78
Steer-roping 56-7, 58-9
Steer-wrestling 58
Stunt riding 66
Suffolk horse 18

Tack 42, 44-5, 50, 63
Tennessee Walking horse 22
Thoroughbred horse 13, 14-15,
  76, 89, 92
Three-day eventing 78-81
Trot 34, 36, 38-9, 77
Turk horse 22
Turpin, Dick 68-9

Uccello, Paulo 28

Vets 50, 52, 81

Walk 34, 36
Welsh cob 17, 91
Welsh ponies 16-17
Western stock saddle 62-3
Wild horses 6-11
Wisping 47
World Show-jumping
  Championships 5, 72, 74, 76, 81